A Light Lunch

A Play

Bridget Derrett

A SAMUEL FRENCH ACTING EDITION

SAMUEL FRENCH

FOUNDED 1830

SAMUELFRENCH-LONDON.CO.UK
SAMUELFRENCH.COM

A LIGHT LUNCH

First performed by the Rolling Stock Theatre Company
in 1999 with the following cast:

Laura Cartwright	Janet Mayo
Richard Cartwright	Sean Mayo
Todd Fellows	David Singer
Henri	Malcolm Ball

Directed by Gill Pegg
Produced by Carol Magill

CHARACTERS

Laura Cartwright; late forties
Richard Cartwright; late forties
Todd Fellows; charming, late thirties
Henri; *Maître d'*, French, fifties

The action of the play takes place in a restaurant

Time — the present

A LIGHT LUNCH

A restaurant. Afternoon

US *is a window looking out on to the street.* DS *of the window is a table with a chair to either side; the table is fully laid for two and has a vase of flowers on it. There is a wine cooler next to the table with a bottle of white wine in it, chilling*

When the CURTAIN *rises, Henri, the* maître d', *carrying two menus, is showing Richard and Laura Cartwright to the table. Richard and Laura are both smart, attractive and stylishly dressed, though Richard's tie is very brightly patterned. He is carrying a briefcase*

Henri It's a pleasure to see you both again.
Laura Thank you, Henri. How are you?
Henri Very well, Mrs Cartwright.
Laura Our favourite table!
Henri Mr Cartwright insisted.
Laura Darling.

Henri pulls out Laura's chair — the L *one — to assist her. Laura and Richard sit*

Henri Might I be so bold as to ask if this is a celebratory lunch?
Richard It certainly is — we're ——
Laura (*interrupting*) — so glad you had a table at short notice. We wouldn't dream of going anywhere else.
Henri A glass of wine while you peruse the menu? (*He takes the bottle from the cooler*)
Laura The Chardonnay ... Richard — you remembered.

Richard Well, it is a special day.

Henri hands the menus to Laura and Richard, opens the wine and pours them a glass each. They do not speak whilst this is going on

Henri I'll leave you for a few minutes.
Richard Thank you, Henri.

Henri exits

Richard and Laura look at the menus. There is a long pause

Laura I do wish you hadn't worn that tie.
Richard What's wrong with it?
Laura What's wrong with it?
Richard Yes …What's wrong with it?
Laura It's just not you.
Richard I thought it was very me actually.
Laura If you want to look as though you're in the middle of open heart surgery it's perfect… At least it won't notice when you drop food on it.
Richard Thank you.
Laura The crab salad looks good.
Richard I thought it was the turquoise one you didn't like?
Laura I don't like that either — I just happen to like this one less…
Richard You always go for crab.
Laura — particularly with that shirt.
Richard Well I'm not taking it off. (*He pauses; pointedly*) You might like to rethink the lipstick.
Laura Why?
Richard It looks like you've been trying to suck a coffee grinder.
Laura You have no understanding of fashion ——
Richard I know what looks stupid …
Laura — or this season's colours.
Richard I think I'll have the avocado.
Laura You know it doesn't suit you.
Richard Have we returned to the tie, darling?

Laura The avocado.
Richard Can we just leave my digestive system out of this?

Henri arrives with bread rolls. He puts them on the table

Henri Everything all right?
Laura Wonderful … We were just saying how nice it is to be back here again.
Henri We've redecorated since your last visit.
Laura I thought something was different … Very nice, Henri.
Henri Would you like some more time?
Laura A few more minutes.

Henri exits

Richard I knew he hadn't forgotten.
Laura Don't be ridiculous …
Richard No — I could see it in his eyes.
Laura You're imagining things.
Richard We should have gone somewhere else.
Laura But we always come here — we've got a history with this place.
Richard That's what I mean.
Laura For goodness' sake; d'you really think that people are tittering behind their menus and saying "He's the one that set fire to the table last year"?
Richard Why don't you say it a bit louder? They didn't catch that over by the toilets.
Laura We'll be ordering from the evening menu at this rate.
Richard The prices have gone up.
Laura It's probably to pay for the new table — and the decorating.
Richard I expect the word went round when I booked.
Laura Yes, they'll have issued a memo to all staff: "Pyromaniac on table ten."
Richard I might have expected you to find it funny.
Laura It was just a minor accident. You always have to make such a meal of everything.

Richard Appropriate, don't you think?
Laura Hilarious.
Richard If you hadn't gone on about the tie.
Laura So now it's my fault. You're the one who waved it over the candle.
Richard I didn't wave it …
Laura I thought you were trying to attract Henri by semaphore.
Richard I was showing you the pattern.
Laura I don't know what on earth you were thinking of buying polyester in the first place.
Richard Put it down to another accident.
Laura I wouldn't dream of having polyester round my neck.
Richard Could I tempt you with a rope?
Laura What?
Richard Nothing … (*Pause*) I notice they haven't got candles on the table today.
Laura It's lunchtime Richard. They put the candles out in the evening. Try not to get paranoid.

Richard gestures off stage to attract Henri's attention

Henri enters

Henri May I take your orders?
Richard Well, I'm ready.
Henri Mrs Cartwright?
Laura Yes … I'll have the mushrooms … No, erm — make that the deep-fried brie … No, wait a minute — I'll try the pâté.

Richard looks exasperated

Henri And for your main course?
Laura The crab salad.
Henri Mr Cartwright?
Richard Consommé followed by the crab salad.
Laura I thought you were having the avocado?
Richard I changed my mind — that's allowed, isn't it?

Laura D'you know, I think I'll have the consommé after all.
Richard For goodness' sake.
Henri Anything else?
Richard Oh — a bottle of still water please.
Henri Thank you.

Henri leaves

Laura Water?
Richard (*sighing*) Yes — water.
Laura You're not expecting to have a bed bath are you?
Richard You make it sound as though I've never swallowed the stuff before.
Laura I suppose it'll be useful if you set fire to the table again.
Richard I'm just trying to indulge in a healthier lifestyle. Look if we're going to argue all the way through lunch …
Laura Sorry. You're right. Today of all days.

Pause

Richard Remember the first time we came here — our very first date?
Laura Henri's father owned the place then.
Richard I spent half my week's wages on that meal …
Laura We thought we were the bees knees ——
Richard I lived on Marmite sandwiches for the rest of the week.
Laura — sitting by the window watching the world go by.
Richard I got the shock of my life when that bill arrived …
Laura You got a shock — I thought I was out with an epileptic …
Richard The chair overbalanced …
Laura All that rolling around on the floor, clutching your wallet — it was so embarrassing.
Richard The woman on table three didn't help …
Laura She thought you were trying to bite your tongue — it was that ridiculous pink tie …
Richard She nearly bloody strangled me.
Laura She thought she was saving your life.

Richard You didn't have a fistful of diamond-encrusted fingers scraping round the inside of your mouth ... If she'd really wanted to help she could have paid the bill.

Pause. They sip their wine

Richard You were wearing that red Crimplene dress.
Laura No ... I don't think it was Crimplene.
Richard My mother had a dress in the same material — not the red, though ——
Laura No ——
Richard — a sort of browny beige.
Laura — it definitely wasn't Crimplene.
Richard I think it was.
Laura I'd know if I'd worn Crimplene.
Richard It's nothing to be ashamed of.
Laura It's like being tattooed, with cellulite.
Richard And your lipstick wasn't quite the same shade of red. I found that rather endearing.

Henri enters, bringing water. He puts the water down on the table, tops up the wine glasses and leaves

Laura It was just before Christmas. You picked me up in your Hillman Minx.
Richard Ah — the good old Hillman Minx. I'd spent all day cleaning it, inside and out ... I used dubbin on the seats.
Laura Yes — I never quite got the seat pattern out of that coat.
Richard We had the à la carte ...
Laura I was so impressed.
Richard That was the mistake; we should have had the set meal.
Laura And we shared a bottle of wine with that other young couple.

Pause

Richard (*sarcastically*) And I shared you with the waiter.
Laura Why d'you always have to bring that up?

Richard Well — for God's sake. The way you were batting your eyelashes it's a wonder they didn't start an avalanche in the Himalayas.

Laura I was not "batting my eyelashes" — I was just having a problem with my mascara.

Richard You'd have had less trouble if you'd Superglued your lashes together.

Laura You were imagining things — as usual.

Richard I didn't imagine leaving on my own while Romeo got his sticky fingers on your red Crimplene.

Laura I've told you — I don't know how many times over the last twenty-five years — but you just won't let it go. I'm fed up with saying it — it wasn't Crimplene!

Henri arrives with the consommé and serves Richard and Laura. They sit in silence until Henri has finished

Henri Enjoy.

Henri leaves

Richard (*raising his glass*) To — "us"!
Laura Yes — of course … To us.

They chink their glasses together

Laura What are we going to do for Lucy's birthday?
Richard Shouldn't we organize a family meal here?
Laura I'm not sure that's what she wants.
Richard But we always come here, for any kind of celebration — you said it yourself.
Laura We always have done — that doesn't mean we have to carry on ad infinitum.
Richard I just thought ——
Laura It is her twenty-first — it ought to be what she wants.
Richard So what does she want?
Laura Well ——

Richard Why do I get the feeling I'm not going to like this?
Laura She's not keen on a party at all.
Richard Not keen?
Laura She'd rather have the money.
Richard Why?
Laura Why do most people want money? To spend it.
Richard On what?
Laura She wants to go — back-packing — around South America.
Richard *Back-packing!*
Laura Don't shout, Richard. People are looking.
Richard Bully for them … They're probably waiting to see if I set
   fire to the table again.
Laura Don't be stupid.

Henri appears

Henri Is everything to your liking?
Laura Delicious, Henri — thank you.

Henri leaves

Richard (*through gritted teeth*) I'm not having a daughter of mine
   traipsing around impoverished countries like some kind of Old
   Age Traveller.
Laura New Age …
Richard Whatever.
Laura She'll be twenty-one — she can do what she likes.
Richard Well, I don't have to contribute.
Laura Don't be so old-fashioned. She just wants to see a bit of the
   world.
Richard Can't she go and stay in a hotel for a couple of weeks?
Laura You're missing the point — as usual.
Richard You should never have bought her that rucksack.
Laura What rucksack?
Richard That blue and red check thing.
Laura She was thirteen …
Richard So?

Laura She was going camping with the Girl Guides. You make it sound as though I bought her an infectious disease.
Richard That's how these things start — it's all subliminal.
Laura I bought you a decent tie twenty years ago — that hasn't filtered through yet.
Richard Other people have normal children — why not us?
Laura You're the man with the tie — you tell me. Anyway, she doesn't want to come here.
Richard How d'you know?
Laura She told me.
Richard But we always come here.
Laura Exactly ... That's why she doesn't want to come here.
Richard What's wrong with it?
Laura It's not the place — it's the — set-up.
Richard Set-up?
Laura The party, the people — you and me.
Richard (*after a pause*) You mean she doesn't want to be seen with us?
Laura She said we always row.
Richard Always row ...
Laura I wish you'd stop repeating everything I say.
Richard But we don't.
Laura We do, Richard — every time we come here we have a row.
Richard Come on — surely not.
Laura All right — you tell me an occasion when we haven't had a row in this restaurant.
Richard Well — er ...
Laura Exactly.
Richard So, that's that then — is it? Overruled.

They finish their consommé in silence

Henri reappears to remove the bowls

Laura That was lovely Henri.
Henri Thank you Mrs Cartwright. I'll pass your comments on to my wife.

Richard I think you might as well bring the champagne over in a minute.

Laura Pushing the boat out, aren't you?

Henri It must be your anniversary?

Richard Sorry?

Henri The celebration. I said to my wife, I'm sure it was this time last year …

Richard Well you'd hardly forget three fire engines and an ambulance for the woman on the next table.

Laura Richard!

Henri Merely a learning curve, Mr Cartwright.

Richard And what did you learn Henri?

Henri To lay fire retardant tablecloths.

Richard Good man. And of course you are right about the anniversary …

Laura (*getting angry*) Richard …

Henri I thought it was.

Richard It is indeed — in fact, our twenty-fifth…

Laura Richard …

Henri Congratulations. I said to my wife: I think this is a special day for the Cartwrights.

Laura Thank you Henri.

Richard And we've treated ourselves to something rather splendid.

Henri Let me guess, Mr Cartwright … A cruise?

Richard Everyone does that …

Henri A new car perhaps?

Richard They look secondhand so quickly.

Laura Richard …

Richard No, give him another chance. I'll add ten per cent to the bill if you get it.

Henri Mmmmmmm … I have it. Property — it must be property.

Richard Wrong!

Laura Can we stop this, please?

Richard To mark the — very — special occasion of our twenty-fifth wedding anniversary, Mrs Cartwright and I have today obtained a — *divorce.*

Henri From each other?

Richard From each other.
Henri I'll get the champagne.

Henri leaves with the soup bowls

Laura Why did you do that?
Richard Why not?
Laura You've embarrassed Henri.
Richard What did you want me to say?
Laura Nothing would have been entirely adequate.

Henri returns with the champagne and opens it during the following

Henri Please accept the champagne with my compliments.
Laura We couldn't.
Richard Yes, we could ... It'll make up for the first bill.
Laura It's very kind of you, Henri.
Henri Not at all ... I think you must be the very first couple to celebrate a divorce at my restaurant.
Laura I wouldn't use it as a selling point.

Henri leaves

Laura You enjoyed that, didn't you?
Richard Well, what difference does it make? We were never Brady Bunch material at the best of times.
Laura It's just that — well — it all started here.
Richard Particularly fitting that it should finish here ...
Laura Very tidy.
Richard Not to mention the cost of our first meal reimbursed via a bottle of champagne.
Laura Cheapskate.
Richard Irony.
Laura You wouldn't know irony if it jumped up and bit you in the tie.
Richard Come on — let's at least make a stab at enjoying ourselves.

Laura Why break the habit of a marriage?

Richard After all it is our last meal together — as a couple.

Laura A sort of Last Supper ——

Richard If I'd just suggested tea and a bun you'd have soon complained...

Laura — a sort of Last Cuppa.

Richard You see, that's always been the problem — you've never taken me seriously.

Laura There wasn't room for two of us in this marriage to take you seriously, Richard.

Richard That's all I wanted — just a bit of respect ...

Henri arrives with the crab salads. He serves Richard and Laura, who sit in silence

Henri leaves

Laura By the way , I'm thinking of changing my name.

Richard Have you got fed up with Laura?

Laura My surname.

Richard Oh — why?

Laura Well, technically I'm not "Mrs Cartwright" any more.

Richard But you've been Laura Cartwright for twenty-five years ...

Laura So?

Richard Everyone knows you as Laura Cartwright.

Laura People soon get used to another name ... If I remarried they'd get used to it.

Richard But what about the children?

Laura What about the children?

Richard Kids get teased when they've got a different surname ...

Laura They're both over twenty, Richard ...

Richard Everyone will know they're from a broken home.

Laura Not so much broken as unstuck.

Richard So what are you going to change it to?

Laura I thought I'd go back to my maiden name — it's the obvious choice.

Richard You are joking.

Laura No. What's wrong with it?

Richard There's nothing wrong with it *per se* — it's just that …

Laura What?

Richard Well … Look at the trouble you had when we first got married. It caused no end of confusion.

Laura You're the one that got in a muddle.

Richard Me and everybody else we knew.

Laura I can't see what the problem is.

Richard Well, if you want to go from Laura Cartwright to Laura Arkwright…

Laura I suppose I could always have a double-barrelled name.

Richard Oh, yes — Laura Cartwright-Arkwright just flows off the tongue.

Laura I don't have to use Cartwright. I could use something else with Arkwright.

Richard Like what? (*Pause*) Oh, no — not his name?

Laura I wish you wouldn't refer to him as though he's the invisible man.

Richard All right — you're not going to use Tad's surname are you?

Laura You know it's "Todd".

Richard He sounds like the Thunderbird that got chucked onto the reject pile.

Laura I wish I hadn't mentioned it now.

Richard You're not the only one.

Richard suddenly cuts off the conversation, grabs the vase of flowers on the table and shields the left (US) *side of his face with it*

Laura What are you doing?

Richard Nothing.

Laura Why are you hiding behind a vase of flowers?

Richard I'm not hiding.

Laura I'm not stupid Richard.

Richard I'm just — enjoying the scent.

Laura Since when did you start inhaling through your left ear. Who's out there?

Laura looks out of the window

Richard For God's sake, Laura — will you stop that?
Laura All right — so who are you hiding from?
Richard If you must know, it's one of Buffy's friends.
Laura So...? (*Pause*) You haven't told her — have you?
Richard Of course I've told her.
Laura Richard, you're a grown man who wants to be taken seriously — and you're cowering behind a table decoration.
Richard OK — so I didn't tell her.
Laura Why?
Richard I didn't think she'd understand ...
Laura What is there to understand? We've been married for ——
Richard (*interrupting*) Were married...
Laura — for twenty-five years. We're celebrating our divorce.
Richard She doesn't like me seeing you.
Laura So where does she think you are?
Richard Business lunch.
Laura Not so far from the truth ...
Richard She's jealous — of you.
Laura She's jealous of me — now there's a thing.
Richard She's only young — it's difficult for her.
Laura Poor lamb ...
Richard Look, I'm not asking for your forgiveness ——
Laura Then you won't be disappointed.
Richard — just that we can stay friends. I know that Buffy isn't your type of person but ——
Laura Hard to believe, isn't it? You'd think that someone who shops like Imelda Marcos, dresses like Scary Spice and speaks like Janet Street-Porter would be just me ...
Richard She wants to be your friend.
Laura Why did I know you were going to say that?
Richard Really.
Laura I must organize another Tupperware party — we'll have a good old-fashioned girls' get-together. Or would Ann Summers be more her bag?
Richard That's what I like about you Laura — you've always been so fair.

Pause

Laura Well, what d'you expect? This is the girl who stole my husband.
Richard Come on, Laura — she didn't exactly steal me. You'd had me marked down at half price for long enough.
Laura Tempted you away, then. I have got my pride, you know.
Richard You've got mine as well — you didn't do badly.
Laura She's just so young. If you'd gone for someone like Judith Chalmers I could have coped.
Richard You did cope. It was probably your finest hour.
Laura Anyway — I don't know why Buffy should be worried.
Richard She's just a bit — insecure.
Laura She's insecure!
Richard I know it's hard to believe.
Laura What does she think I'm going to do — seduce you over a light lunch and arrange a flight to Las Vegas?
Richard I didn't mean ——
Laura We're not Taylor and Burton, you know. Once is quite enough.
Richard I know ... It's just ——
Laura If I'd wanted another ride on the rollercoaster I'd have kept the same seat.
Richard Yes ... Very clever.
Laura Anyway — what's she going to do?
Richard Who?
Laura The girl — her friend — she's hardly likely to rush off and phone Buffy straight away.

The sound of bleeping emanates from Richard's jacket pocket. His pager has gone off

Laura What's that?
Richard What's what?
Laura That sound — you're bleeping.
Richard No, I'm not.
Laura Yes, you are — what is it ...?

Richard Nothing.

Laura You haven't had a pacemaker fitted, have you?

Richard Of course I haven't.

Laura I knew she'd be too much for you.

Richard It's a pager.

Laura A pager.

Richard Yes ... (*He pulls the pager out of his pocket and switches it off*) A means of communication.

Laura I know what a pager is, Richard. What I want to know is why you've got one.

Richard So I can be contacted — for business purposes — and stuff — in an emergency.

Laura But you sell life insurance ...

Richard So ...

Laura *Double Indemnity* was just a film ... Nobody needs emergency life insurance, Richard; at least if they do I'd check they haven't got a one-way to Glasgow on the six-fifteen.

Richard All right — all right.

Laura Let's have a look.

Laura snatches the pager from Richard and looks at it

Richard Laura!

Laura It's got a little message on it.

Richard (*sarcastically*) That's because it's a message pager.

Laura Oh darling ... You're right — someone does want you ... (*She reads from the pager*) "Call me Buffy". I didn't know you gave them names.

Laura passes the pager back over to Richard

Richard (*reading: pointedly*) "Call me — Buffy."

Laura (*sarcastically*) Oh, I see. Buffy wants to speak to you. I wonder why.

Richard I told you her friend had seen me. (*He takes a mobile phone out of his jacket pocket and taps in a number*)

Laura (*as Richard dials*) I wonder what it was that made you stand out — the table decoration you were wearing, or the tie?

Pause

Richard (*into the phone*) Is there a problem, Heart?
Laura Heart!
Richard (*twisting round in his chair so that he is not facing Laura; into the phone*) Did she? ... Well — yes ... actually. ... Look, it's a bit difficult. ... No. ... No. ... Of course not. (*He twists round further still and talks confidentially to Buffy*) To be honest, she was rather upset, so I felt I ought to — you know — sit her down somewhere. ... I knew you'd understand. ... Yes. ... I'll leave the mobile on. Love you. (*He hangs up and turns back to his meal, replacing the 'phone in his pocket*)
Laura So — how is *Buffy*?
Richard I do wish you wouldn't say her name like that.
Laura Well for goodness' sake... What kind of a name is "Buffy"? She sounds like a synthetic chamois-leather.
Richard She was named after the singer, if you must know.
Laura What, Buffy Hardcastle, Wrexham's answer to Kathy Kirby?
Richard Buffy Saint Marie.
Laura Buffy Saint Marie — come on!
Richard There was a bit of a mix-up. Her mother thought she was the singing nun.
Laura Now that is what I call irony. A perfect example of the genre.
Richard Perhaps this was a mistake.
Laura What — Buffy?
Richard Lunch.
Laura Sorry.

There is a long pause; they continue eating

Laura We came here for dinner the day we moved into The Gables.
Richard (*remembering the occasion fondly*) Yes — I'd pulled a muscle in my back helping the removal men.
Laura I told you not to interfere — but you wouldn't listen.
Richard Some of the stuff was bloody heavy.
Laura You only moved the artificial Christmas tree and a hostess trolley.

Richard At least I did something — I didn't notice you doing anything.

Laura Oh, you mean apart from making tea and sandwiches for everyone with a small child strapped to my back, another welded to my leg and a labrador on heat shackled to my left wrist.

Richard Yes — well — I was in a lot of pain.

Laura I couldn't believe you'd let them carry you up the garden path on the dining-room table.

Richard Not just pain — agony. Anyway they got a tip.

Laura They deserved one. They weren't hired to transport live-stock.

Richard It felt a lot better after a hot bath. I was looking forward to a meal out.

Laura My parents babysat and we got all dressed up ...

Richard You wore that black velvet dress...God you looked good in that dress.

Laura I'd made it myself ——

Richard Really special.

Laura — a Vogue pattern.

Richard You couldn't tell — that you'd made it yourself, I mean. You made me feel proud to be with you.

Laura It's the only time you've worn a tie that I've picked for you.

Richard Was it?

Laura Don't you remember? I hid all your ties in one of my kitchen boxes — you couldn't find a single one.

Richard Oh yes ... Then you produced a "moving in" present. It was a good night.

Laura Until we tried to leave.

Richard You always make it sound as though it was my fault — I couldn't help my back seizing up.

Laura At least nearly everyone had gone by then.

Richard It was probably sitting in the same position for a couple of hours.

Laura Of course, I knew somebody would see us — they always do.

Richard If it hadn't been for the two girls on the table by the door ...

Laura Another memorable departure.
Richard A stroke of luck, really …
Laura That dreadful Delia Cheek from the WI was driving past with her husband as the taxi arrived.
Richard I mean, you don't expect to find two female wrestlers just when you need them …
Laura Word had spread through the Institute by the end of the next day.
Richard I wouldn't have thought they could have lifted me ——
Laura Borne aloft on a restaurant chair ——
Richard — but they did.
Laura — like Julius Caesar on a commode ——
Richard They were strong girls ——
Laura — being transported down to the Tiber for his ablutions.
Richard — yes they were strong — I'll give them that.
Laura I had to sit next to the taxi driver while you lay flat out on the back seat; it must have looked like I'd been picked up by him for a bit of late-night fun. All grist to the WI mill.

Pause. Richard refills their glasses with champagne

Laura You haven't tried the water.
Richard What? Oh . . . Well — I've sort of gone off the idea now.

Pause. They continue eating

Richard (*pensively*) It was worth it — wasn't it?
Laura What?
Richard Us.
Laura You mean today?
Richard No — I mean the last twenty-five years.
Laura Our marriage.
Richard Yes.
Laura (*uncertainly*) Of course it was.
Richard You don't sound sure.
Laura It's just such a funny question. We can't undo twenty-five years. It's happened It's gone. We have to move on.

Richard I know ... I just ... Oh, forget it.

Laura Look ... We had a marriage, a home, children. We had a life together. It wasn't all bad.

Richard Great ... I feel a lot better.

Laura You just don't like the idea of having failed.

Richard That's not fair ...

Laura I think our marriage was just one of those that had a shelf life.

Richard I do miss you ...

Laura You miss having me around because we've got memories...

Richard It's not just that — we spar off each other.

Laura We argue — we've always argued.

Richard We used to call it "lively discussion".

Laura We only called it that for other people's benefit — the children, our parents — it was still arguing, whichever way you looked at it.

Richard Yes — well. I don't get any of that now.

Laura What — from Buffy?

Richard Yes. She doesn't know how to.

Laura So what happens if she doesn't agree with you ... ?

Richard She just shrugs her shoulders.

Laura There must be something that irritates her — surely?

Richard No ...

Laura Not even your ties?

Richard Particularly not my ties ...

Laura Then you should enjoy a very happy and peaceful old age.

Richard What about — Todd?

Laura I suppose we don't argue, come to think of it.

Richard Not at all?

Laura No ...

Richard Oh.

Laura We laugh a lot.

Richard So did we.

Laura Did we? I must have missed it.

Richard I thought we had fun.

Laura It was the sense of humour.

Richard What sense of humour?

Laura Exactly.

Pause. They finish their lunch

Henri arrives

Laura That was lovely, Henri.
Henri Would you care to see the menu again?
Laura Er — not for me. I know I'd be tempted …
Richard Same here. I'll just have a coffee.
Henri Mrs Cartwright?
Laura Yes … I'll have a coffee … Thank you.

Henri clears away the plates. Richard and Laura sit in silence

Henri exits

Richard That's not like you.
Laura What?
Richard No pudding.
Laura We're going out tonight.
Richard Oh.
Laura Todd and I.
Richard I assumed ——
Laura A sort of — celebration.
Richard Freedom of the city?
Laura Well — you know …
Richard Where are you going?
Laura We thought we'd try that new Italian restaurant in town.
Richard Yes — I've heard it's very good.
Laura I didn't think it would be right, coming here — with Todd.
Richard No … Well, I haven't brought Buffy here of course.
Laura Of course.
Richard We're staying in. Buffy's preparing a surprise meal.
Laura So you're celebrating as well?
Richard Yes — yes, I suppose so.

Pause

Laura I'm pleased you're happy — really.
Richard Well — I ...
Laura You are, aren't you?
Richard It's not the same ...
Laura How could it be?
Richard If we could just turn the clock back ...
Laura And which argument would you like to go back to?
Richard Is that how you'll remember us?
Laura I'm only looking forward now.
Richard Perhaps we could make this an annual event.
Laura (*gently*) Let go, Richard ...
Richard What?
Laura Let go.

Pause

*Henri arrives with the coffee and two brandies, plus the bill on a
plate. He puts everything down on the table*

Henri (*of the brandies, before Richard can say anything*) On the
house, Mr Cartwright.

Richard takes a glass and raises it to Henri

Henri leaves

Richard It's been fun.
Laura I wouldn't have had it any other way.

Richard and Laura touch their glasses together

Richard I'll do a cheque for Lucy.
Laura She'd like that.

Richard takes out cash and places it on the plate with the bill

Richard D'you think we've been coming here longer than any
other couple?

Laura I wouldn't be at all surprised.

Richard Actually I reckon there's a couple in here today that are having an illicit meeting.

Laura You mean apart from us.

Richard I mean a — clandestine lunch.

Laura What makes you think that?

Richard Well, don't suddenly stare — but there's a car parked over the road that's been there almost since we arrived.

Laura Where?

Richard Blue BMW. There's a chap reading a paper in the driver's seat. He keeps looking over.

Laura I know ... (*Pause*) It's Todd.

Richard It's Todd!

Laura Yes.

Richard What's he doing there?

Laura Waiting for me.

Richard For God's sake. You mean he's been sitting there all through our meal?

Laura What's wrong with that?

Richard I don't like being stared at by some gigolo while I'm having lunch with my wife.

Laura I think the phrase you're searching for is "I don't like being stared at by my ex-wife's boyfriend while I'm having lunch".

Richard Doesn't he trust us?

Laura He knew I'd have a couple of glasses of wine, so he said he'd take me home.

Richard But I was going to get a taxi ... I thought I'd drop you off.

Laura You don't have to look after me any more, Richard — there's somebody else to do it.

Pause

Richard Have the kids met him?

Laura Yes — and before you ask: yes, they like him.

There is the sound of a car door closing outside

Richard Well — you've always had good taste. Oh God — he's coming over.
Laura Just behave yourself.
Richard There isn't going to be some sort of "handing over the wife" ceremony, is there?

Todd enters and walks across to the table

Laura Darling.

Todd bends down and kisses Laura. Richard gets up

Richard We haven't met ...
Laura No, of course — I'm sorry ... Todd, this is Richard; Richard, Todd. Where have I heard that?

Richard and Todd shake hands

Todd Laura's told me a lot ——
Richard — about me ... Yes — well — I hope some of it was good.
Todd I think we'd better get a move on.
Laura (*looking at her watch*) Oh, is that the time? Just give me five minutes, darling.
Todd I'll wait in the car. Nice to meet you, Richard.
Richard I'm equally thrilled — Todd.
Todd Oh — great tie.

Todd leaves

There is an awkward pause

Laura You couldn't help yourself, could you?
Richard It was when you called him "darling".
Laura You'd know all about that wouldn't you — "Heart".
Richard All right, all right. Anyway — why the rush?
Laura We're off to the travel agents ... last-minute holiday.
Richard Oh.

Laura So I'd better make a move.
Richard Before you go ...

Richard opens his briefcase and takes out a carefully wrapped present

Laura What's this?
Richard Open it — you'll find out.
Laura I hope you haven't gone and bought something expensive.
Richard It's a reminder — of twenty-five happy years.
Laura Mmmmmm.

She takes the present and unwraps it to reveal a pile of gaudy ties

What?
Richard All the ties you've loved to hate.
Laura I don't understand.
Richard Did you honestly think I liked wearing this lot?
Laura Are you saying ... ?
Richard It was the pink tie.
Laura The pink tie?
Richard The night the waiter took you home.
Laura You mean that's what all this is about — twenty-five years of tie torture?
Richard It just started as a joke — but you always took it so seriously, I couldn't quite help myself.
Laura So you've always known?
Richard I have a supply of very nice ties at work... I changed into them every morning when I arrived and changed back before I left.
Laura Rat.
Richard I only wore the pink tie because my mother had bought it... I hated that tie... Then, when you went home with the waiter ——
Laura I didn't go home with the waiter.
Richard Well, you went off to the kitchen with him...
Laura He got me a brandy... I was in shock after your break-dancing display on the floor.

Richard But you said ——
Laura No I didn't — you assumed and you played the wounded
  lover so well it seemed a shame to put you right.

Pause

(*Laughing*) What am I going to do with this lot?

Pause

Richard So ...
Laura So ...
Richard You will keep in touch?
Laura Of course; after all — the children...
Richard Yes — well — good luck.

Richard kisses Laura on the cheek

Laura exits

*Richard closes his briefcase and puts it on the floor. He sits down
at the table and replenishes his glass with champagne. He looks out
through the window*

We hear the car doors open and close and the car drive away

Henri enters

Henri Well, Mr Cartwright?
Richard It was worth a try, Henri. But...

*Henri sits at the table and pours some champagne into Laura's
glass*

Henri Mrs Cartwright — she is still enamoured with Mr ...Todd?
Richard It would seem so. But things change ... There's always
  next year.

Henri You have agreed to meet again?
Richard Not yet — but she will. So you'd better save our usual
    table, Henri, and make sure you have the Chardonnay on ice.

Henri and Richard touch their glasses together and drink

Henri What now Mr Cartwright?
Richard Now, Henri — I have a date with Tie Rack.

CURTAIN

FURNITURE AND PROPERTY LIST

On stage: Table laid for two, with vase of flowers
Wine cooler with bottle of white wine in it
Other tables (optional)

Off stage: Two menus (**Henri**)
Briefcase containing carefully-wrapped present of gaudy ties (**Richard**)
Plate of bread rolls (**Henri**)
Bottle of water, more bread rolls (**Henri**)
Two bowls of consommé (**Henri**)
Bottle of champagne (**Henri**)
Two crab salads (**Henri**)
Tray with two cups of coffee, two glasses of brandy and bill on plate (**Henri**)

Personal: **Richard**: pager, mobile phone

LIGHTING PLOT

Practical fittings required: nil
A restaurant. The same throughout

To open: General interior lighting

No cues

EFFECTS PLOT

<table>
<tr><td>Cue 1</td><td>Laura: " … yes, they like him."
Sound of car door closing outside</td><td>(Page 23)</td></tr>
<tr><td>Cue 2</td><td>Richard looks out through the window
Car doors open and close; car drives away</td><td>(Page 26)</td></tr>
</table>

www.ingramcontent.com/pod-product-compliance
Ingram Content Group UK Ltd.
Pitfield, Milton Keynes, MK11 3LW, UK
UKHW021820150726
7214IPUK00017B/239

Alternative Accommodation

a play

Pam Valentine

Samuel French

www.samuelfrench-london.co.uk
www.samuelfrench.com (US)

CHARACTERS

Anna, recently widowed; 70s
Peter, Anna's son, high-powered financial consultant, full of
   self-importance and highly unaware; late 40s
Joy, Anna's daughter, runs her own PR company, dashes
   through life to show how super-efficient she is; 40s
Gemma, Anna's daughter, vicar's wife, lives in the country
   and has never quite left the sixth form; late 30s to early 40s

The action takes place in Anna's house

Time — the present

AUTHOR'S NOTES

   The play can be set very simply against a black backdrop or
curtains.
   Place names that appear in this text, for example Watford
and Waterloo, can be changed to suit the location of production.
   Anna's, Peter's, and Joy's mobile phones must have differing
ring tones.

Pam Valentine

ALTERNATIVE ACCOMMODATION

The living-room of Anna's house

UC is a table or cabinet with a tray holding a bottle of whisky and tumblers. On either side of the table/cabinet there are two dining-room chairs facing DS. There is an armchair DL and another DR. Both armchairs are of simple construction and are not necessarily matching

A doorbell rings long and loud

Anna (*off, calling*) I'm coming! (*Slight pause to allow her to open a door*) Hallo, dear. Come on in.

Anna and Joy enter R. Anna is wearing a dressing-gown and slippers. Joy is wearing a very smart trouser suit and a white shirt. She carries a shoulder bag and a document case

(*As she enters*) Have you been ringing for long?
Joy Ages. I was getting really worried. Are you all right, Mum?
Anna I'm fine, dear. I was asleep.
Joy Asleep? You never sleep in the daytime.
Anna I know, but I had a late night, woke very early, made a cup of tea, took it back to bed and ... (*She looks at her watch*) Oh my goodness — is that the time? I'll pop up and get dressed. Let the others in for me when they get here.

Anna crosses L, as Joy looks at the armchairs

Joy Mum — where's the three-piece suite?

Anna (*hardly pausing*) What?
Joy The three-piece ——
Anna (*glancing back*) Oh, I got rid of it.
Joy Got rid of it? Why did you …?

Anna exits L

Joy is obviously puzzled. She puts her bag and document case by the dining-room chair R. *A mobile phone rings. She takes a phone from her bag*

(*Into the phone; briskly*) Joy Webster. … Mr Godwin, hallo. … Yes, I'll be with you by two. … Yes, with a strategic over-view and a draft communication plan of the whole concept. … Well, if you don't — but I'm sure you will — it's back to the drawing-board. But I think you are going to be very excited when you see the layout. … Sorry? ... Ah, if anyone from the media does ring pass them straight over to me. …

The doorbell rings

Yes, absolutely. See you later, bye. (*She switches off the phone and returns it to her bag*)

She exits R

(*Off*) Oh! Both of you together, come on in.

Joy enters followed by Gemma and Peter. Gemma is flustered and breathless. She is wearing a raincoat and sensible shoes. She carries an umbrella, a small holdall and a handbag. Peter has an officious manner. He wears a business-suit and has a mobile in an outside pocket

Gemma I'd just got off the bus and I saw Peter's car at the traffic lights. So I ran and knocked on the window.

Peter Knocked! (*To Joy*) She nearly smashed it in with her umbrella.

Joy (*to Gemma*) You're not staying, are you?

Gemma Staying? No, course not. (*She puts her holdall, bag and umbrella on the floor by the armchair* R)

Joy (*indicating the holdall*) What's in there?

Peter Where's the three-piece suite?

Gemma (*looking in the holdall*) My knitting, my flask ——

Joy She's got rid of it.

Peter Why?

Gemma My book … (*She takes the book out*)

Joy She didn't say.

Peter That's a bit worrying, isn't it?

Gemma What is?

Peter Mother's got rid of the three-piece suite.

Gemma (*looking round*) Oh yes…

Peter Anything else gone?

Joy I've no idea! Would you like me to go round and take an inventory?

Peter Where is she?

Joy Upstairs, getting dressed.

Peter Getting dressed?

Joy She was asleep when I arrived.

Peter Asleep? She never sleeps in the daytime.

Gemma Is she ill? I could stay if she's ill. I always carry a toothbrush and spare knicks.

Joy Too much information, Gemma. (*To Peter*) She looked OK to me. She said she had a late night.

Peter Doing what?

Joy I don't know! Stop interrogating me.

Gemma (*offering Joy the book*) This is really good. Do you want to borrow it?

Joy I don't have time to read books. (*Glancing at it*) Especially books with a nurse on the cover. (*To Peter*) Listen, before she comes down, how do you think we should go about this? Chit chat chit chat or jump straight in or what?

Peter I've no time for chit chat, Joy, no time at all. Which is why
  I've made a note of … (*He reaches into an inside pocket*)

Peter's mobile phone rings

  (*He sighs impatiently*) Here we go … (*He takes out his mobile
  phone; into the phone*) Webster. … In that case make my three
  o'clock my four o'clock and switch my five o'clock to ten o'clock
  tomorrow. … Got that? … Right. (*He puts the phone back into his
  pocket and reaches again into an inside pocket. He takes out a
  folded piece of paper*) Bullet points.
Gemma What points?
Joy Bullet points.

Gemma looks blank

  The main things we want to say.
Gemma (*making a mental note*) Oh. I see. Bullet points.
Peter (*unfolding the paper*) This couldn't be happening at a worse
  time—end of the fiscal year, corporate clients going crazy … (*He
  looks at the paper*) My secretary's on maternity leave.
Joy (*sarcastically*) Is that a bullet point?
Peter No. But very irritating.
Gemma Is it her first?
Peter First what?
Gemma Baby!
Peter I don't know. (*He looks at the paper*) Right. One — it's three
  months since dad died. Two — to keep a house this size on is
  financial madness. Three — we should organize the sale of this
  place and find suitable alternative accommodation. Four —
  investing the equity to give her an income.
Joy You're not going to come out with it all just like that, are you?
  Bam bam bam.
Peter No, of course not.
Joy Good.
Peter But neither am I going to waste time going all round the
  houses. We've made the plan and now we execute it.

Gemma Andrew said she might not want to move.

Peter If Andrew was a financial consultant and not a vicar he'd realize she's going to have to move. Apart from anything else what's going to happen when something goes wrong? Which it will in a house this age and size. I can't come racing over here every time a washer needs changing. And I don't want her to prey to every cowboy workman who knocks on the door.

Gemma (*hesitantly*) I've been thinking ——

Joy Always dangerous.

Gemma I know we didn't discuss it but … (*She hesitates*)

Peter (*warily*) What have you been thinking, Gemma?

Gemma Well — suppose she lived with us.

Joy Which one of us had you in mind?

Gemma Not one of us all the time. We could split her up. Three months with each.

Joy That's nine months, Gemma, three threes are nine.

Gemma Oh. Four months then.

Peter Four months? I couldn't ask Jen to take that on board! I mean she's fine about the odd weekend and a week or two in the summer but with all her committee work … She's just taken the chair of the Pewter Mark Society.

Gemma looks at Joy

Joy Don't look at me. I run my own company twenty-four-seven. I don't have time for cosy chats and making milky drinks.

Peter Let's agree right now that living with any one of us is not an option. I mean think about it ——

Joy I don't have to think about it. No.

Gemma Andrew said we'll have a job persuading her to move. I mean how long has she lived here? Forty years? (*To Joy*) You're forty-five ——

Joy Forty-four, actually.

Peter (*getting tetchy*) How long she's lived here is completely irrelevant. The important factor is she can't go on living here. Dad's pension is now halved, I've done a breakdown of the running costs and ——

Gemma I think we should give her the chance.

Joy Chance of what?

Gemma Living with us. It would make her feel wanted.

Peter What's the point of making her feel wanted when she's not wanted! Well ... Of course she's wanted but ... haven't you listened to a word we've just said?

Gemma Yes, but we could tell her we'd thought about it then — sort of explain why she can't.

Peter Suggest something that isn't possible to make her see that it isn't possible? Brilliant.

Gemma There's no need to be sarky!

Joy Oh, for God's sake, Gemma. Last week, — and with great difficulty — I cleared a morning so we could all meet and decide what was the best course of action. Why didn't you say anything about her living with us then?

Gemma It was the Mothering Sunday service, Andrew gave all the little ones a daffodil to give to their mummies and — I know I'm a soppy old thing — I got a bit weepy and I thought, well, I thought perhaps we could share her.

Joy If you want to clear your conscience and have her to live with you then fine. But count me out.

Gemma Oh, not permanently, Joy. Just the three — four months. It would have to be in the summer because Andrew said ——

Peter And what happens in the other eight months?

Gemma Well, if she can't come to either of you ——

Joy And she can't.

Gemma Perhaps she could — go on one of those old people's holidays.

Joy For eight months? She'd need a bloody big suitcase.

Peter Gemma, living with us is out of the frame and please — please, Gemma, don't mention it.

Gemma looks huffy

She has two options — a retirement home ——

Joy I did say last week I'm not sure about that. I can't see Mum sitting in a high-backed chair with a pink bow in her hair.

Peter Or ——

Gemma They're not all like that. Andrew visits a home where the choice of activities is amazing. Flower arranging, yoga, singalongs ——

Peter Or we find a suitable apartment in a retirement development. God knows you see the signs for them wherever you go. Low maintenance, communal garden ——

Gemma Suppose she let some rooms?

Joy Now what are you talking about? Let some rooms where?

Gemma Here! If she had an income from that she could stay.

Joy Oh get real — how could she cope with lodgers?

Peter Who would have to be interviewed and have references checked …

Gemma It's an option!

Peter No, it definitely isn't an option and if you're going to come out with these stupid top-of-the-head suggestions we'll get nowhere. We stick to what we've agreed and I don't want you muddying the water with an idea that can't be ... what's that whisky bottle doing there?

They all look at the whisky bottle

Joy It's a cold day, perhaps she thought we might like a glass.

Peter She always makes tea.

Gemma (*with the voice of doom*) Oh dear …

Joy Oh dear what?

Gemma Getting rid of the furniture, sleeping in the daytime, drinking whisky — could be the first signs of dementia.

Peter What!

Joy (*to Gemma*) Why must you always turn everything into a drama.

Gemma It can come very suddenly. Andrew takes Holy Communion to a lady who's only fifty-five. One week she was serving school dinners and the next she couldn't remember where she lived.

Peter Oh my God ——

Joy (*to Peter*) Calm down. There's probably a perfectly logical explanation for all those things.

Gemma I don't think she could live with any of us if she's got dementia.

Peter How many more times? She's not living with any of us with or without dementia.

Gemma She'll be very upset. Us telling her we think she ought to move. I'm feeling quite wobbly actually.

Joy (*indicating the whisky*) Have a drop of that.

Gemma No, thank you. (*She smiles in a smug and annoying way*) Andrew's praying for us.

Joy Now why does that depress me ...

Gemma Because you think it clever to be cynical about God. And prayer.

Joy (*innocently*) Cynical? *Moi?*

During the following, Anna enters L. *She is wearing slippers, a dress, and a jacket or cardigan with a pocket*

Peter Oh, stop it, both of you. We need to keep calm and remain focussed here. Otherwise there's no point in our ... Mother!

Anna Hallo, everyone! I'm so sorry I wasn't here to greet you. Did Joy tell you I overslept?

Peter (*first kissing her cheek*) She said you had a late night?

Anna Oh, late for me, not for you. (*She moves towards Gemma, stops and looks down*) Well, silly old me. All this time getting ready and I've still got my slippers on. How did that happen?

Anna kisses Gemma. Peter and Jo exchange nervous glances

How was the journey, Gemma? Trains on time?

Gemma (*setting in for long discussion*) Well, there was a delay at Watford, we all had to get out on to the platform — no-one told us why — and ten minutes later we all had to get back on. And then when we got to Waterloo ——

Joy Nice dress, Mum. Is it new?

Anna Do you know I was thinking when I put it on? Did I buy this before your father died or after? And I couldn't remember.

Gemma looks at Joy and shakes her head

Anna Why don't we all sit down? (*She sits in the armchair* L)

Gemma puts her raincoat over the back of the armchair R *and sits. Joy pulls the dining-room chair* R *forward and sits in it. Peter stands* C *as if conducting a meeting*

Peter (*slowly as if talking to a child*) We were wondering about the three-piece suite, Mother?
Anna What about it?
Peter It isn't here any more, is it?
Anna No.
Peter Can you remember what you did with it?
Anna I told Joy. I've got rid of it.
Peter Right — and can you remember why you got rid of it?
Gemma Was it because Daddy had his stroke in the armchair?
Anna Did he? I'd forgotten that. Let me think … (*She gets slightly upset*) Oh, dear, I must have had a reason, mustn't I?
Joy Of course you must, Mum, don't worry about it.

Joy shakes her head at Peter signifying to him to stop talking about it

Gemma When you — if you get rid of anything else Andrew's got several refugee families moving into the parish and they'd be so grateful for anything you're throwing out.
Anna I'll remember that, Gemma. (*She looks from one to another*) It's lovely to see you all but I've been wondering and wondering … Why did you all want to be here together?

Joy and Gemma look at Peter

Peter Well, the thing is, Mother, the reason we're all here together there are one or two things that we feel we need to ——

Joy's mobile phone rings

Joy Damn. (*She takes the phone from her bag; into phone*) Joy
   Webster. ... Mr Godwin, hallo again. ... May I stop you there?
   You have been supplied with all the relevant data to back up that
   survey. ... Press launch! What press launch? (*She mouths "sorry"
   to the others and rises*)

Joy exits UR

Anna Peter?
Peter I think we'll wait for Joy to finish her call.
Anna There isn't a problem with the will is there? I haven't heard
   anything from the solicitor.
Peter No, that's progressing smoothly. All the paperwork's in and
   it's just a case of ——

Peter's mobile phone rings. He takes it from his pocket

(*Into the phone*) Webster. ... (*He sighs impatiently*) Then make
   the ten o'clock the four o' clock and shift the four o'clock to
   eleven o'clock. ... (*Suddenly alarmed*) What off-shore funds?

Peter exits UL

Gemma They're a great intrusion, aren't they, mobile phones?
   There was a woman next to me on the train and her phone rang five
   times in thirty minutes and I thought what did people do before ...
   Oh! I said I'd let Andrew know I'd arrived. (*She takes a mobile
   phone from her handbag and keys in a number*) It's ringing. Oh
   dear, it's the answerphone. I do hate having to ... (*Into the phone;
   slowly and deliberately in a special telephone voice*) Hallo. It's
   me. I've arrived. I will ring you from the station. Oh! From the
   station when I get back not when I get here because I'm already
   here. Oh, you know that, don't you because I've already said I've
   arrived. Bye-bye, God bless. (*She returns the phone to her
   handbag, looks at Anna and leans forward conspiratorially*)
   Now, tell me, how are you really, Mummy?

Anna Oh, I'm muddling through, I suppose. One day at a time

Gemma Andrew was saying there must be times when you feel all topsy-turvy.

Anna He's right about that. There are definitely times when I feel all topsy-turvy.

Gemma Andrew has a bereavement group once a week. People say it helps so much to talk through their grief. There might be something like that around here?

Anna Yes, there might.

Gemma Sometimes there's a notice in the doctor's surgery.

Anna Is there?

Gemma It'll be there with all the other notices. You know, have you got arthritis, are you incontinent, don't smoke if you're pregnant. That sort of thing.

Anna Thank you, dear. I'll know where to look.

Gemma Andrew said you can ring him anytime you want.

Anna That's very kind of him.

Gemma Oh! And he's made a list of some lovely quotes for Daddy's stone. Or have you thought of an inscription yourself?

Anna I've thought of several but I haven't finally decided on ——

Joy enters R. *She goes to her document case*

Joy That man is permanently set to "mega" panic.

Gemma I was just asking Mummy about Daddy's stone.

Joy (*looking in the case*) What?

Gemma Daddy's gravestone. Has she thought of a nice inscription?

Joy Oh, yes. Look, sorry, I must just check something. (*She sits* R *and looks through papers*)

Peter enters L *with his mobile phone*

Peter (*as he enters; into the mobile phone*) Tell him it's imperative that he does that. … Imperative. … Vital then, do you understand vital? Tell him it's time to kick the brick. … Brick! (*He puts his phone away*) One brain cell and I get her. Sorry about that, Mother.

Anna If you've all finished your phone calls why don't we have a
   cup of tea? The tray's all ready. (*She rises*)
Peter Er — let's have one later, when we've had a bit of a chat.
Anna If that's what you want. (*She looks from one to the other*)
Peter The thing is, Mother, the thing is … (*He looks at Joy*) Joy?
Joy (*rifling through papers*) Yes?

Peter takes the folded paper from his inside pocket

   Sorry. (*She closes her document case*)
Gemma Those are his bullet points.

Joy raises her eyes to heaven

Peter The thing is, Mother, it's been three months now since —
   since you lost Dad and ——
Gemma I always think that's a funny expression. Losing someone.
   Because I mean you don't exactly "lose" them do you? It isn't as
   if you don't know where they are? Andrew always says people
   shouldn't be afraid of the word "death".
Joy I don't expect they are until they're dying.
Gemma That's the whole point, Joy, if people would think about
   it before they die they wouldn't be so ——
Peter Do you want me to speak or not?
Anna Well, I certainly do.
Peter Thank you. It's been three months since Dad …
Anna Died.
Peter Yes. And naturally we're very concerned about you.

Joy and Gemma make assenting noises

Anna I can see you are and that's very kind but all things considered
   … Well, I seem to be managing.
Peter At the moment, yes. But this is a big house, a very big house,
   which needs considerable upkeep. And in my — in our opinion
   to continue living here on a reduced pension would be financial
   madness. Two can live as cheaply as one but one cannot live as
   cheaply as two.

Gemma He means although the food bills are less the other bills remain the same. Like gas, and electricity and ——

Joy For goodness sake, Gemma! Mum isn't stupid.

Gemma I was simply trying to ——

Peter Excuse me? Please? Thank you. (*He looks at his notes and mumbles through the previous words until he reaches the right place*) Ah, yes. And we have to bear in mind, Mother, that you are not getting any younger.

Gemma You've made your three score year and ten, Mummy. That's good isn't it?

Anna Is it? I'm beginning to wonder …

Peter Therefore having fully reviewed and made a comprehensive breakdown of the financial situation it would seem sensible for you to consider a move.

Anna (*instantly alarmed*) Move? From here?

Gemma Andrew said you wouldn't want to.

Peter So we all got together and discussed the situation fully.

Joy We've really thought about it, Mum.

Peter And we think we've come up with a sensible solution. Don't we, girls?

Joy Absolutely.

Anna Move … Oh dear … That's a big step.

Gemma Poor, Mummy, you've lived here such a long time, haven't you?

Anna Where would I go?

Peter That's why we got together to discuss the possibilities and ——

Gemma We talked about your living with us, Mummy.

Peter and Joy look at Gemma in disbelief

Anna Like Auntie Joyce did when Frank died, you mean? A few months with one then a few months with another?

There is controlled alarm

Peter We did consider that, Mother, of course we did, but in all fairness to you — it wouldn't work, would it?

Anna It's working for Auntie Joyce.

Joy You wouldn't want to come to me, Mum. You'd have a miserable time, I'm out most days from eight till eight and anyway I don't think you'd enjoy life ten floors up.

Anna Yes, but there's a lift and I'm used to my own company.

Joy looks worried

Peter And of course Jen and I discussed your coming to us ——

Anna Oh! It's always luxury staying with you, Peter. *En suite* bathroom, beautiful garden, shops just a walk away.

Peter Yes. Those are the pluses, yes. But on the negative side we are away a great deal and ...

Anna I could look after the house for you.

Peter Far too big a responsibility, I wouldn't have an easy minute, Mother.

Anna Gemma? I love your village, such friendly people.

Gemma Well, I think you'd be fine with us during the summer but Andrew's worried about the winter. We get very snowed in. And suppose you slipped? And broke a leg, or a hip, or — something. And we had to call an ambulance — and it couldn't get through the snow?

Anna Yes, that could be a problem — so, if I can't live here and I can't live with you ... (*She looks distressed*)

Joy (*feeling remorseful*) It's not that you can't live with us, Mum, it's just that with work and all our commitments ——

Gemma Andrew says I work harder than he does. Last year when he had flu and it was the Harvest Supper everyone said that——

Peter Bottom line, Mother, we do all live very busy lives.

Anna sits for a moment in silence, looking into space. Gemma gives Joy an anguished look. Joy shrugs her shoulders. Peter looks at his watch. Anna sighs then looks at them

Anna So, what do you think I should do?

Peter Right. (*He clears his throat*) After much consideration we
  have decided that we should sell this house, find you alternative
  accommodation, invest the remaining equity thus ensuring you of
  an income to supplement any pensions to hand and … And …
  Well, that's it really.
Gemma We'd find somewhere really nice. We wouldn't want you
  to be unhappy.

Anna is silent

Joy Mum?
Anna Oh, sorry. But — it's a bit of a funny feeling to think of you
  all getting together to talk about me.
Joy It wasn't exactly "talking about you" it was knowing that things
  had to be sorted and you couldn't be expected to cope with it all
  on your own.
Peter We wanted to clear the dead wood, prepare the ground, then
  lay it all before you.
Anna I see. Well, you'd better tell me about this "alternative
  accommodation"?

They all relax

Peter Right, as we see it there are two options. A retirement
  home ——
Anna Retirement home!
Gemma Some of them are really lovely, Mummy. You have your
  own room and you can take some of your own furniture. And there
  are lots of activities. There's always something going on!
Joy If you don't like the sound of that, Mum, we could think about
  a retirement development.

Anna looks puzzled

You'd have your own apartment, your own front door, but there'd
always be someone there if you — had any little problem.

Gemma And some of them have activities!
Joy Oh do shut up about "activities".
Peter So what do you think, Mother?

After a few moments' thought, she rises and goes to the table/ cabinet. She stands half-turned away from them and pours some whisky into a tumbler

Gemma Are you feeling wobbly, Mummy?
Anna I'm not sure how I'm feeling. (*She drinks*) Oh, how rude of me, would anyone ——

They all make noises and gestures of dissent

Peter Do you drink a lot of whisky, Mother?
Joy For God's sake, Peter ...
Anna A lot ... (*She considers*) No, not a lot.
Gemma Was it the strain of nursing Daddy that started you off?
Anna I really can't remember. It might have been. I usually have one in the evening, about sixish.
Gemma But it's only twelve o'clock.
Peter Is it? We'd better push on.
Gemma Don't rush Mummy, Peter. I expect she wants a little time to mull things over.
Peter Understood. But assuming we're all agreed on the basic premise and as we're now into March I don't think we should hang around. Let's get our diaries out and pencil a meeting here in say— how long do you think you'll need to — er — mull, Mother? One week? Two?

Anna turns to face them. She is no longer a slightly bewildered old lady. Her manner is decisive and controlled

Anna I don't need any time at all.
Peter Excellent! Right— two-pronged attack. We put the house on the market, gather in all info on suitable retirement developments ——

Peter's mobile phone rings. He takes it out of his pocket

Anna (*in a very firm voice*) Switch that off.
Peter But ——
Anna Switch it off. And sit down.

Startled, Peter switches the phone off and sits on the armchair L

One thing puzzles me, why is it that suddenly I'm old and frail and need looking after?
Peter (*to the others*) Now that's not what we meant, is it?
Joy Of course not.
Gemma We only want to help.
Anna But you didn't hold a conference about how to help when your father was ill. Daily visits to a hospital miles away, then nursing him at home for six months, you assumed I was perfectly capable of doing all that. Now — suddenly — this house is too much for me, I'm not getting any younger, and I should sell up and shift into the twilight zone.
Gemma We didn't mean it to sound like that, Mummy.
Anna Then I wonder why it did?
Peter This is all based on your financial situation, Mother.
Anna I'm sure it is. But it's also based on giving you three the least worry about me, isn't it?
Joy That isn't fair, Mum. We'll always worry about you wherever you are.
Anna But I don't want to be worried about. I just want to get on with my life. And because of that I have made some decisions. In fact I've been "mulling" things over for quite some time. Since long before your father died. So here are my bullet points. Yes, the house will become a financial drain and yes, I am selling it. But no — and again no — I am not going to a retirement home no matter how many activities there are and neither am I going anywhere where you press the bell for matron if you have a headache.
Gemma I think if you looked at some ——

Anna I'd still feel the same. Oh! And to stop you all worrying; no, I haven't got dementia.

The other look alarmed

I got rid of the suite because it was nineteen years old and I never liked it; I was asleep when you got here because I had a late night, and I'm drinking whisky because I like it.

They stare at her

I bought this dress last week and I kept my slippers on for fun. (*She indicates the ceiling*) I was only up there and for once I was glad your father would never have fitted carpets. (*She takes a drink, looks at her glass and tops it up*)
Peter You heard us talking.
Anna Every word.

There is a brief embarrassed silence

Joy We wanted — want to help.
Anna Then you should have talked to me not to each other. A very irritating thing happens when you get old. People talk at you, and about you, but never to you.
Peter I apologize for all of us if we've offended you, Mother, but the financial facts still have to be faced.
Anna They are being. I'll tell you how in a minute. But first I'd like to say a few words about your father.
Gemma Ah — that's nice.
Anna You asked me, Gemma, if I'd thought of an inscription for your father's gravestone. How about "He came with nothing, he gave nothing, he left with nothing"?

Puzzled, they consider her words

Gemma Is that in the Bible?

Anna No. I thought of it myself because it sums up his life in a sentence. (*She pauses then speaks slowly and deliberately*) Your father was a very difficult man.

Gemma Mummy! That isn't fair, he was old and ill.

Anna Which made him worse. I'm talking about long before he was ill. I'm talking about what he was like through all our years together. Mean, selfish and opinionated. A difficult man I could have coped with but a difficult man who enjoyed being a difficult man, that was something else again. He treated me as if I was stupid until I thought I was stupid. Only in these past months have I realized how good life can be. What is it couples say now? "We drifted apart"? We were never together in the first place.

The others all look at each other. Obviously stunned

Joy I don't understand — why did you get married? Something must have attracted you to him.

Anna Yes. His moustache.

Peter You married my father because you liked his moustache?

Anna Yes. I thought it made him look like a film star. And two months after we got married he shaved it off. By which time, Peter, I was expecting you.

Joy But — if you were so unhappy why did you stay? You could have left him?

Anna Till death do us part, Joy. I'd made my vows and I kept them. Every one.

Gemma Andrew always says ——

Joy Oh spare us, Gemma, please.

Peter I'm sorry if he wasn't the — ideal husband, but he was a very good father.

Anna If you mean you were fed, clothed and educated, yes, he was. But other things? Think about it for a moment. (*She counts on her fingers*) No noise, no friends home, no television, no fun in the garden, no fun on the beach — in fact — no fun ever. Shall I go on or are the memories coming back?

Gemma This isn't fair. He isn't here to defend himself.

Anna He couldn't if he was.

Joy Oh, come on, Gemma — admit it. It was Mum we had all the good times with, it was always a minefield walking round Dad. That's why we all left home as soon as we could.

Peter He wasn't the easiest of men, I agree, but he always made sure Mother had a comfortable life.

Anna Did he? A three-storey house with no help of any kind. Keep all the bills for him to check? No independence? Never allowed to learn to drive? I'm having my first lesson next week.

Peter In a car?

Anna It always helps.

Gemma Can you learn to drive at your age?

Anna Oh yes. A man walks in front with a flag.

Joy I'm sorry you had such a rotten time, Mum, I really am but hearing you say all this — it's a bit of a shock.

Anna I'm sure it is. And I didn't intend to say any of it but when you sat there, the three of you, making it so patently obvious that not one of you is prepared to have me living in your house, that hurt.

They are all unable to look at Anna

Not that I would have lived with any one of you. How could I live in your house, Peter, with an appalling snob who fills her life and her house with worthy women who spend most of their time comparing how much they pay their cleaners. You, Joy, are so determined to be voted businesswoman of the year you are completely forgetting how to be a woman. Do you have to dress like a man? And Gemma — you no longer have an original thought in your head. "Andrew says, Andrew thinks, Andrew feels." What do you say and think and feel?

Gemma Oh!

Joy As a matter of fact ——

Peter Let's all stay calm here. And try and forget the very hurtful things mother has just said. She obviously isn't at all herself.

Anna As a matter of a fact I am very much myself. At last.

Peter You say you're going to sell the house ...

Anna Actually it's sold.

Peter Sold? Sold?

Anna Your father used to repeat himself. You want to watch that.

Joy Who to?

Anna To whom, Joy, to whom. A property developer. He's going to turn it into self-contained luxury apartments. Really gorgeous apartments. I was quite tempted to stay here and live in one.

Peter You have sold this house without a word to any of us? I'm a financial consultant!

Anna I'm not stupid, Peter, I knew the market value of this house. And when I found out how much they wanted it I added another ten thousand.

Gemma Mummy! Was that honest?

Anna As honest as they were when they said they didn't really care if they bought it or not.

Peter And exactly how much money is this property dealer giving you?

Anna Lots. Lots and lots and lots.

Joy (*laughing*) You sneaky old thing! Well, we'd better get together and arrange what you're going to do with all this money. Where you're going to go. I've got a day I could clear next week …

Gemma Next week's difficult for me. Andrew's dedicating the new kneelers and the Bishop's coming the week after …

Peter I'm at a conference the week after …

Anna You don't have to worry about getting together. I know where I'm going.

Peter (*warily*) Where? Or is that a secret as well?

Anna Not at all. I'm going to Florida.

Joy
Peter   ⎫(*together*) Florida!
Gemma

Anna Yes. Florida. (*She looks at Gemma*) No problems getting an ambulance through the snow there.

Peter But … But … But — it's all swamps and alligators.

Anna As your father was incontinent for the last three months of his life and snapped my head off every time I changed the sheets I'm used to swamps and alligators.

Joy I need a drink.

Joy moves to the table/cabinet and pours herself a whisky

Gemma (*weakly*) So do I. (*She moves to the table/cabinet*)

Joy pours another whisky

Peter Florida! That's in America!

Gemma You won't know a soul, Mummy, you'll be so lonely.

Anna I don't think I will. (*She drinks*) Harry's moving out there as well.

Peter (*rising*) Harry? Who the hell is Harry?

Anna Harry. I met him in the library. I'd dropped my ticket and he picked it up. We started chatting, then we had a cup of coffee, and he kindly came round and changed my washer. Just as well because you wouldn't have wanted to come racing round, would you, Peter?

Joy (*to Peter*) You asked for that.

Peter And what do you know about this — Harry, apart from his plumbing skills?

Anna He's a widower, he's my age, he used to own a garage. (*She smiles*) And he's got a moustache …

Gemma Mummy, you're not well. (*To the others*) She's not well.

Anna And he calls me Anna.

Peter But—that's your name! (*To Gemma*) You're right, she's not well.

Anna Your father always called me Annie. When he called me anything. It's so lovely to hear my proper name. And Gemma, I'm perfectly well. And I'll be even better when I'm sitting on my balcony in the sun looking down at the pool.

Peter And this Harry is going to be there with you on the balcony, is he?

Anna Certainly not. If we lived together I'd lose my pension, wouldn't I?

Peter Er — yes.

Anna Never again will I be in a position where I have to ask a man for money. He'll have his front door and I'll have mine.

Gemma How long has this been going on?

Anna I met him the week after the funeral.

Gemma The week after — I don't know what Andrew's going to say.

Peter moves to the table/cabinet, picks up the whisky bottle and holds it high

And I suppose he introduced you to this, did he?

Joy Oh, put it down, you look ridiculous.

Gemma Andrew's going to be very, very, very shocked.

Anna Why? I think I should give a talk to his bereavement group It might give them a bit of hope.

Gemma Some people like to take time to grieve.

Anna And believe me so would I take time if I had anything to grieve about. Till the very last minute I never stopped hoping your father would change and become a loving man. Even at the end when I sat by his bed for hours and hours, if he had just once said one kind thing ... "Thank you" would have been enough ... (*She sighs*) So now I have found a loving man I am going to enjoy every minute. Because as you've pointed out, Peter, I'm not getting any younger.

Peter Just a minute. This — place in Florida ...

Anna It's a condominium. That's what they call apartments out there.

Peter Presumably it's costing less than the lots and lots of money you're getting for this house ...

Anna Much less.

Peter So with the outstanding equity ——

Anna I'm thinking of buying a race horse.

Peter's jaw drops. Anna laughs

I'm going to ask you to invest it for me.

Peter sighs with relief

Gemma But, Mummy, you could be buying a pig in a poke! You haven't seen it — you haven't ...

Anna Yes, I have. I flew back last night. That's why I was tired this morning.

Joy (*finding it funny*) You flew to Florida! You!

Anna Did you really think I was fool enough to buy it without seeing it?

Gemma (*longingly*) Did you say it's got a pool?

Anna Yes. Well, I hope you'll see it when you come out. If you book your flights on the internet you'll get a very good deal. Oh! That's another thing — we can email each other.

Peter Email? Email?

Anna Yes.

Joy But you can't ... (*She looks at Anna*) Or can you?

Anna Only basic literacy so far but I'm coming on.

Joy You knew why we were coming here today, didn't you?

Anna I had a pretty good idea, yes.

Peter Then why let me stand there and go through all ... (*He makes hand gestures*) All that.

Anna Oh, I suppose it was in the hope — the vain hope — that you might have asked me what I wanted to do and where I might like to go and just — make me feel wanted. Instead of a problem that had to be dealt with.

They stand, heads down, like three naughty children

Oh, for goodness' sake — cheer up! And start looking forward to fun in the sun. There's a golf course, Peter, and a church for you and Andrew, Gemma. It looks like a meringue and the vicar wears a white tuxedo but it's still a church.

Joy Anything for me, Mum?

Anna Yes, shops full of dresses. Now, I'm having copies made of all the legal papers, just so you can see everything's in order. The packers are coming on May the first and anything I don't want I'll send to you, Gemma.

Gemma What for?

Anna Your refugee families.

Gemma Oh yes.

Anna And if there's anything you want you must say. Any little thing to remind you of your father? (*She looks from one to the other*)

They are all silent

Well, have a think. Now — what about that tea? Or coffee?
Peter (*looking at his watch*) Sorry, Mother, but now my three o'clock's my two o'clock …

Anna looks at Joy

Joy I really should pop back to the office …
Anna Gemma?
Gemma Actually, Mum, there's a PCC meeting tonight and if Peter drops me at the station I can …

A mobile rings. They are puzzled as no-one recognizes the ring tone. Anna takes a phone from her pocket. The three are now look in complete shock

Anna (*into the phone*) Hallo? … (*Her voice warms*) Oh, hallo. … (*She laughs*) Me too. I was still asleep when Joy arrived. … Yes, they're all here. … Yes, I've told them. … Well, a bit of a shock naturally but … (*she looks at their unsmiling faces then smiles to herself*) they're all very happy for me. … Oh, what a lovely idea, that would have been nice —— (*She looks at the others*) Harry wanted to take us all out to lunch. (*Into the phone*) I'm so sorry I'm afraid they can't spare the time. … (*She looks at them as she speaks*) I know, but you see, they do all live very busy lives …

Curtain

FURNITURE AND PROPERTY LIST

On stage: Table or cabinet. *On it*: tray with bottle of whisky and tumblers
Two dining-room chairs
Two armchairs

Off stage: Shoulder bag containing a mobile phone; a document case (**Joy**)
Umbrella; small holdall containing a book; handbag containing mobile phone (**Gemma**)

Personal: **Anna**: watch; mobile phone
Peter: mobile phone; folded piece of paper

LIGHTING PLOT

Practical fittings required: nil. 1 interior. Same throughout

To open: General interior lighting

No cues

EFFECTS PLOT

Cue 1   As the play opens   (Page 1)
Doorbell rings long and loud

Cue 2   **Joy** puts her bag and document case by the chair R   (Page 2)
Joy*'s mobile phone rings*

Cue 3   **Joy** " ... pass them straight over to me. ..."   (Page 2)
Doorbell rings

Cue 4   Peter reaches into his pocket   (Page 4)
Peter*'s mobile phone rings*

Cue 5   **Peter** " ... we need to —"   (Page 9)
Joy*'s mobile phone rings*

Cue 6   **Peter** " ... paperwork's in and it's just a case of ..."   (Page 10)
Peter*'s mobile phone rings*

Cue 7   **Peter** " ... on suitable retirement develoments ..."   (Page 16)
Peter*'s mobile phone rings*

Cue 8   **Peter** switches the phone off   (Page 17)
Cut mobile phone ring

Cue 9   **Gemma** "... Peter drops me at the station I can ..."   (Page 25)
A mobile phone rings

9 780573 023729